ADVANCED KICK BOXING

THE CUTTING EDGE

Pat O'Keeffe

CHIEF INSTRUCTOR MOD-KA KICK BOXING

CHIEF INSTRUCTOR MOD-KA KARATE-JUTSU

HEAD AND BRITISH TEAM COACH (K.I.C.K.)

SUMMERSDALE

Copyright © Pat O'Keeffe 2002

The right of Pat O'Keeffe to be identified as the author of this work has been asserted in accordance with sections 77 and 78 of the Copyright, Designs and Patents Act 1988.

No part of this book may be reproduced by any means, nor transmitted, nor translated into a machine language, without the written permission of the publisher.

Summersdale Publishers Ltd
46 West Street
Chichester
West Sussex
PO19 1RP
UK

www.summersdale.com

Printed and bound in Great Britain

ISBN 1 84024 181 0

Acknowledgements

My grateful thanks to my assistant instructors Chris Keeliher and Frank Duffy for helping demonstrate the techniques in this book, and to my wife Cathy for the photography. Also many thanks to Kelly, my editor at Summersdale, for all her wise words and guidance on the production of this book.

About the Author

Pat O'Keeffe is the British head and team coach for the American kick boxing organisation, K.I.C.K. A regular commentator on kick boxing for Sky Sport and a renowned authority on the subject, he has fought three World Champions.

Contents

Introduction

The aim of this book is both simple and ambitious: to take a ring fighter and turn him into a world champion.

To that end it will define what it takes to become the best – the king of the hill. It will set out the necessary qualities, skills and mindset of a champion and map out how to achieve world status over a measurable timeframe.

Such goals, regardless of natural talent, are never easy and call for ruthless self-examination and hard sacrifice; to be a champion you have to make space in your life to grow, to become something other than just another fighter.

It means being physically stronger, attaining additional techniques, becoming mentally sharper, acquiring the tactics and strategies that create the opportunities to win, and having the determination to discipline yourself over the three to five years necessary to launch a world title bid.

Finally, it means growing as a person and realising that within you there is the potential to be a world champion. You have to start by appreciating the size of the mountain that you have to climb and then visualising your success. That means positive thinking and positive action married to a desire that is so strong it burns a hole in you.

If you have opened this book looking for a quick fix and a shortcut to glory, then close it now, for the road to a world title is littered with undisciplined dreamers. But if you have the potential and the genuine will to be a champion, then it will ask the relevant questions and reveal the answers that can turn the average ring fighter into something special.

Can this book make you a world champion? Not on its own. For this book is not an A to Z, but a compass. It can point the way, but you have to walk the miles.

The book is divided into five parts. Each part is intended to reveal a key area of fighting skill. You are advised to read, experiment, test and review all information contained within this book to obtain the maximum benefit.

This is the third book in the series. The first, *Kick Boxing – A Framework for Success*, dealt with the sport of kick boxing from novice to intermediate level – if you have not read it, then do so now. It will ensure that you have covered the basics necessary for you to launch your championship bid and you will find it the perfect primer for this book.

The second book, *Combat Kick Boxing – Realistic Self-Defence*, dealt with the street applications of this martial system and for the first time took the skills of kick boxing out of the ring. Many people are attracted to kick boxing because of its apparent realism; *Combat Kick Boxing* shows just how effective it can be when your life is at stake.

Together, all three books form a series aimed at producing the holistic kick boxer – fit, trained and briefed, from novice to champion, from ring to rumble. No other series of books has ever before attempted to define this dynamic martial system in this way. Use each as intended: to teach, to reveal and to act as a working reference.

Part One: Advanced Kick Boxing Techniques

Part One of this book aims to examine in depth kick boxing techniques used at an advanced level of ability. It will define and explain the areas of skill under examination and lay out a series of exercises and drills that will help you gain that skill, or if you possess it already, to gain a greater insight into that technique's full potential. The explanations and demonstrations are not the last word. That has to be supplied by you – experimenting and adding your own experience to the matrix and then taking it into the ring.

The Bolo

The bolo is a looping punch that gains its power by whipping in at the last moment. This whipping in is called 'shortening the arc'. The bolo can be thrown in any plane (the angle through which the punch travels). This makes it an extremely versatile and powerful tool.

The name 'bolo' was appropriated by Hispanic boxers to describe a particular punch that was thrown in a long, looping manner reminiscent of the swing of the bolo, a long-bladed knife used by Filipino field workers. The knife is swung in a circular fashion and was used to deadly effect by Filipino guerrilla fighters against the Japanese during the Second World War. Because of its origins, this punch is rarely, if ever, found in standard boxing or kick boxing texts.

For the purposes of explanation, I will only describe three planes through which the bolo can be thrown – the horizontal bolo, the rising bolo and the looping bolo. (The other planes are all the angles in between and can be found by a little thought and experimentation.)

The Horizontal Bolo

A horizontal bolo superficially resembles a loose hook, but a hook gains its power by an explosive twist of the ankle, hip and shoulder, whereas a bolo depends on shortening the arc of the punch's loop. (Diagram 1)

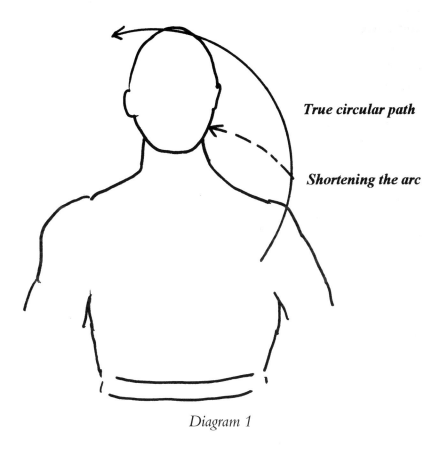

True circular path

Shortening the arc

Diagram 1

Even the long-range looping hook, which is thrown with a wide action and lots of body commitment, is not the same as a bolo. This is because the long-range hook follows a true circular path.

The horizontal bolo, however, goes outside the opponent's line of vision and then cuts back by shortening the arc. How much you cut back depends on you – for at literally any point on the true circular path, you can cut back, thereby making the bolo very hard to read. It is very effective for going around an extended or loose guard. (Figs. 1 and 2)

Fig. 1   *Fig. 2*

Straight jabs and crosses can be linked into a deadly combination with bolo punches, causing your opponent to constantly vary his guard against the speed of the straight punches and unpredictable path of the bolo.

This technique is of particular interest to a small fighter up against a big, strong opponent. To gain the maximum effectiveness, the small fighter should work his way inside, bury his head on his opponent's chest and then whip horizontal bolos around the guard. (Fig. 3) The effect on your opponent is stunning, with punches seeming to come from nowhere.

At medium and close ranges the horizontal bolo can be thrown by dipping your body to avoid an attack and then launching the bolo from the dipped position. (Fig. 4) Because of the tendency for your opponent to follow your body movement with his eyes, the bolo arcs home unobserved. Targets for the horizontal bolo are the jaw and the temple.

Note that there is less commitment of the body with a bolo than with most punches. This is because the whipping motion accelerates the punch and does not require body weight behind it to produce power. That said, a good technician always aims to up the percentage of body weight in a punch because it increases the punch's destructive power. The increase of body weight into a bolo is a good starting point for the advanced fighter's own experimentation.

Fig. 3

Fig. 4

The Rising Bolo

At first glance the rising bolo resembles a loose uppercut, but an uppercut, like a hook, requires an explosive twist of the ankle, hip and shoulder. The rising bolo is a good tool for the long-limbed fighter who has to find a solution to a smaller opponent continually attempting to take the fight to close quarters or an opponent who continually ducks low.

Because its action is large, the timing of the rising bolo is crucial. Throw it as your opponent steps forward. As he presses in, take half a pace backwards with your rear foot. Throw your rear hand in a loop until it reaches your hip. Now shorten the arc and whip the punch in under the ribcage. (Figs. 5 to 7)

Targets for the rising bolo are the chin, the floating ribs, solar plexus, heart and liver.

Warning: The heart is a particularly dangerous target for any punch. A strong blow can throw out the heart's rhythm, causing a fighter serious distress. It is never a technique to be used lightly.

Practise the rising bolo on focus pads until you learn to swing loose and whip in. Tightening up or tension will kill the technique. After practising on the focus pads start to compare it with the uppercut – the feel of each is very different, as is the type of power generated.

Fig. 5

Fig. 6

Fig. 7

The Looping Bolo

The looping bolo is thrown over the top of a guard or an incoming punch. In this respect it resembles an overhand cross, but the shortening of the arc makes it much harder to read. It is a stunning blow, appearing to come from nowhere and striking with real force. (Figs. 8 and 9)

Fig. 8   *Fig. 9*

It is an ambush technique that is especially effective against a weak, ill-timed or unvaried jab. It requires good timing, distance appreciation and a honed sense of anticipation.

To practise the looping bolo, have your partner throw jabs at you whilst holding an angled focus pad in his rear hand. As he throws the jab, whip the bolo over the top of it, dipping your body as you do so. (Fig. 10)

The perfect moment to throw the looping bolo is halfway through your opponent's jab. As with the

Fig. 10

horizontal bolo you can increase the deception ratio by dipping your body as you throw the punch. (Fig. 11 and Diagram 2)

The crossover point between a horizontal and looping bolo becomes blurred at this point, as indeed it does with most refined skills. The important thing to remember is to isolate each of the three basic bolos until you have achieved a reasonable level of competence in them, then experiment with differing planes, dipping and timing. Variety will keep your opponent guessing.

Fig. 11

Diagram 2

The Bolo as a Counter

Because deception is built into the delivery of the bolo, it is a devastating counter-attack. Below are some examples of its use:

Counter to a Front Kick

As your opponent throws a rear leg front kick, take a pace to your left with your front foot and angle away from the kick. Throw a looping bolo with your rear hand and strike his temple. (Figs. 12 and 13) Good timing is required with the side step. Move too early and your opponent will follow you with the kick.

Fig. 12

Fig. 13

Counter to a Right Cross

As your opponent throws the right cross, slip to your left and launch a rear hand horizontal bolo at his chin. (Figs. 14 and 15) This is a fast, powerful and very hard-to-read counter. It also works against a southpaw jab. It is a very good counter for a close-range fighter. Note that good head movement will tempt your opponent into throwing shots or disturbing his guard to meet the perceived threat. This is the perfect moment to throw this counter.

Fig. 14

Fig. 15

Counter to a Left Jab

As your opponent throws the jab, step diagonally forward with your right foot and launch a horizontal bolo. (Figs. 16 and 17) The path of the bolo will take it between your opponent's gloves and seem to come from nowhere. Good anticipation is required and again, good head movement should tempt your opponent into throwing a 'go-away' jab, leaving him open for the ambush.

Fig. 16

Fig. 17

Counter to a Right Hook

As your opponent throws a right hook, duck the punch and bob and weave to your left. Now throw a rising bolo to his liver, solar plexus or chin. (Figs. 18 to 20) Your opponent is prevented from seeing the rising bolo by his own punching arm and the counter will rise between his guard. This is a strong counter that will shake up your opponent and unsettle his decision-making ability. Nothing subdues an opponent more than being punished with a heavy counter.

Fig. 18

Fig. 19

Fig. 20

Counter to a Left Hook

If your opponent is a short-range, clubbing-type puncher, then this counter is extremely effective at throwing out his rhythm. As your opponent throws a left hook at your head, bob and weave to the outside and throw a strong left rising bolo at his heart. (Figs. 21 to 23)

The jolt to his system is impressive and will leave him in disarray for anything from a few seconds to a minute. Seize the chance to launch a heavy combination using straight and round, body and head, and hand and leg shots to overwhelm his defences.

Fig. 21

Fig. 22

Fig. 23

Summary

Bolo punches can be thrown with greater subtlety than any other punching technique. This is because you can:

1) Alter the plane (angle) of attack.
2) Alter the degree of whip (shortening of the arc) in each delivery.
3) Add a dipping evasion of the body.

In a fight you can quite literally alter each and every bolo you throw by including just enough variation of angle to defeat your opponent's guard or incoming attack. As with all techniques you should allow time for the skill to develop. Practise it against less proficient fighters in the gym, gradually increasing the variety of angles and the different types and grade of fighter that you use it against. The first time an opponent in the ring should realise you possess a subtle and deadly bolo is when it explodes on his chin. Good hunting!

Jumping Kicks

Jumping kicks are the province of the expert kicker and as such are a natural area of study for a prospective champion. The value of jumping kicks lies in the fact that you can deliver near-maximum body weight behind the technique.

Jumping kicks work best as a jack-in-the-box, that is, a technique that pops up unexpectedly. When this surprise element is combined with maximum weight the result will be a man-stopper.

There are dangers to using jumping kicks. You are very vulnerable on landing and can be swept heavily. The very nature of the kicks means you make large expansive body movements that can be easily read by your opponent if you do not time or disguise them correctly.

Lastly, never experiment with jumping kicks in the fight ring. Work your chosen techniques in the gym until they are second nature and make sure to include focus pad, big bag and sparring practice in your training schedule.

It is especially important to work on timing. You are recommended to have a partner spar with you at half speed so that you can practise the correct moment to launch your jumping kick.

Jumping Rear Leg Roundhouse Kick

Jumping rear leg roundhouse kicks are versatile and fast. They work best as a counter to any technique thrown from your opponent's rear side. This is because by throwing a rear side technique your opponent has to open up target areas particularly suitable for the jumping roundhouse kick.

Counter to a Right Cross

As your opponent throws a right cross, pull your left side back and jump. At the peak of your jump twist to your right and throw a jumping rear leg roundhouse kick to the side of his head. (Figs. 24 to 26)

Fig. 24

Fig. 25

Fig. 26

The power comes from a strong hip twist that should be emphasised throughout the technique. The natural action of the kick takes you out of the path of the right cross and if your opponent telegraphs his intent, you can knock him out with this technique.

Practise this on the big bag by swinging it away from you and just as it starts to return, pull back, jump and twist. Try to explode through the bag and make it jump rather than swing away from you. Three sets of ten at the end of your gym workout should maintain a good skill level.

Another way to practise this is to have your practice partner hold a shield with his left arm and wear a glove on his right. As he throws the right cross, perform the jumping roundhouse counter. (Fig. 27) This develops good timing and anticipatory skills.

Fig. 27

Counter to a Roundhouse Kick

As your opponent throws a roundhouse kick to your body, pull your left side back and perform a jumping rear leg roundhouse kick. (Figs. 28 and 29)

By throwing a roundhouse kick at you he has turned and therefore opened up his target areas. Good anticipation and opponent awareness will help you trigger the counter before he can execute his own roundhouse kick.

Fig. 28

Fig. 29

Attacking with a Combination

When attacking with jumping kicks it is vital that you either time them well or build the kick into a combination, so that the kick flows naturally out of the action. The combination shown here works because there are straight punches, a jumping roundhouse kick and a low sweep that will force your opponent to switch his priorities rapidly as the combination is released.

1) Throw a left jab to the face. (Fig. 30)
2) Throw a right cross to the face. (Fig. 31)
3) Throw a rear leg sweep to his leading leg. (Fig. 32)
4) Jump and throw a jumping roundhouse kick to his face. (Fig. 33)

The aim of the sweep is to dislodge your opponent's front foot and pin his weight so that he is off-balance and vulnerable to the jumping roundhouse. The loss of balance also prevents him launching a counter.

Fig. 30

Fig. 31

Fig. 32

Fig. 33

Jumping Spinning Heel Kick

This kick generates so much power that it can rip right through any but the strongest of guards. Being technically advanced with large, expansive movements and a requirement for pinpoint timing, this kick is the hardest of all to land cleanly, but when you do it produces the most spectacular of knockouts.

A description of the basic technique is given below:

> **1)** Jump straight up and twist at the top of the jump. (Fig. 34)
> **2)** Bring your knee up high. (Fig. 35)
> **3)** Bring your leg around in a circular arc, keeping the leg straight throughout. (Fig. 36)
> **4)** Make contact on the target area with your heel. (Fig. 37)

Ensure that you twist your head, shoulders and body – particularly the hips – throughout the technique. The best time to throw the jumping spinning heel kick is as a counter to any straight punch or kick from your opponent's lead side.

Fig. 34

Fig. 35

Fig. 36

Fig. 37

Counter to a Jab

As your opponent throws a jab, jump and spin into the kick, contacting the side of his head with your heel. (Figs. 38, 39 and 40)

Even experienced fighters will occasionally 'scissor' their jab – that is, allow their right guarding hand to move backwards as they throw a jab. (Fig. 41) This provides the perfect opportunity to power in your counter.

Practise this by having your training partner hold a shield on his right arm and throw a jab at you with his left. The instant you see movement from his lead hand, jump and spin into the technique. (Fig. 42)

As always, the big bag is the tool for building knock-out power. Practise until you can hit the bag with genuine speed and power and then do three sets of ten at the end of each gym session to maintain your skill level. It is also important to give time over to practise on the focus pads as this will hone your accuracy and timing.

Fig. 38

Fig. 39

Fig. 40

Fig. 41

Fig. 42

Counter to a Lead Leg Front Kick

As your opponent throws a lead leg front kick, perform a lower parry and jump into the counter. (Figs. 43 and 44)

The kick can be performed without the lower parry, but the parry has the added advantage of disrupting your opponent's balance and turning his target areas towards the arc of the kick. It will be extremely difficult for him to mount an effective guard against this counter. It is truly stunning. The best way to practise this counter is to have your opponent hold a kick shield as he throws the kick. (Fig. 45)

Fig. 43

Fig. 44

Fig. 45

Attacking with a Combination

Any combination that pins your opponent on the back foot is tailor-made for a jumping spinning heel kick finish. The combination shown here is a standard one and consequently there is nothing about the opening techniques that suggest a jumping kick is coming. To that end, it is important to work on a smooth flow from one element of the combination to the other.

1) Throw a jab. (Fig. 46)
2) Throw a right cross. (Fig. 47)
3) Throw a left hook to the head. (Fig. 48)
4) Throw a jumping spinning heel kick to the head. (Fig. 49)

Fig. 46

The three-punch opener will destroy his guard and balance, allowing you to commit totally to the blistering finish. Practise this combination on the focus pads. Work for speed, power, accuracy and, not least of all, flow.

Fig. 47

Fig. 48

Fig. 49

Advanced Kick Boxing

Summary

1) Timing is vital with jumping kicks. A cold kick thrown without thought is an invitation to disaster.

2) Jumping kicks work best as counters or as part of a combination.

3) Train on the big bag for power, the focus pads for accuracy, and the shield for mobility and situational work.

Sweeping

The foot sweep is a throw achieved by knocking one or both of your opponent's feet from under him. In *Kick Boxing – A Framework for Success*, elementary sweeping techniques and principles were dealt with. Here we will go into more depth with a range and variety of sweeping methods.

Some of these sweeps are subtle and call for sensitivity to your opponent's balance. Ideally you should practise with a partner until you can pick the technique out of nowhere. You are strongly recommended to work on one sweep or combination sweep until it is sharp and you are able to use it successfully in sparring. Half-learned techniques serve no purpose and under the pressure of a ring contest, could see you getting knocked out. Practised until second nature and used intelligently, however, there are no finer techniques than sweeps for robbing your opponent of his confidence and his ability to plan and execute effective techniques and tactics.

Timing lies at the root of good sweeping. You should sweep before his weight has come to rest as his foot lands following a kick or a step. Anticipation married to fast reactions will enable you to sweep with confidence and disrupt your opponent's preparations.

This is of particular importance when confronting a heavy puncher who wants to close and deliver crippling body punches and strong hooks to the head, or a heavy kicker who does not follow on with hands after throwing a shot.

There should be strong commitment of the body behind a sweep and plenty of follow-through with the leg. Sweeps work best as counters or as part of a combination.

Because the rules of most kick boxing organisations require sweeping to be 'boot to boot', it is not possible to show all types of sweeping techniques, although those shown below are extremely effective and combine readily with other techniques into a fighting combination.

Sweep/High Roundhouse Combination as a Counter

The aim of this combination is to trap your opponent's weight on his rear leg and then smash home the high roundhouse.

1) As your opponent throws a lead leg front kick, move back. (Fig. 50)
2) The instant his foot lands, throw a heavy basic sweep at his lead leg. (Fig. 51)
3) Follow immediately with a roundhouse kick to the face. (Fig. 52)

Fig. 50

Fig. 51

Fig. 52

If your initial sweep is powerful enough it will disrupt his balance and his guard will instinctively widen to regain balance, thus leaving an opening through which to drive the high roundhouse kick. By sweeping you also take his concentration low, so by using a high follow-up attack you have a very good chance of success.

I have some spectacular video of two breathtaking knockouts achieved by my fighters with just this combination. Sweet and simple, it deserves study.

Sweep/High Roundhouse Combination as an Attack

1) Throw a fast jab. (Fig. 53)
2) Follow with a heavy right cross. (Fig. 54)
3) Now move through the sweep. (Fig. 55)
4) Finish with the roundhouse kick to the face. (Fig. 56)

The basic jab/cross combination is shown because it is simple to perform and lends itself to many types of follow-up combinations; however, the above attack can work just as well off a right cross.

Practise this on a six-foot bag so that all elements of the attack can be exercised, and then work it in sparring sessions to develop the timing. Experiment with different openings that lead into the combination sweep/ kick.

Fig. 53

Fig. 54

Fig. 55

Fig. 56

Lead Leg Front Kick/Sweep as a Counter

1) As your opponent throws a right cross, throw a lead leg front kick stop-hit. (Fig. 57)

2) Move in fast and throw a deep sweep to his back leg with plenty of follow-through. (Fig. 58)

The stop-hit works because in order to throw the cross, your opponent has to turn towards you, thus exposing his body to a snap lead leg front kick. If delivered strongly enough this will jar him and make him very vulnerable to the sweep.

Heavy punching close-range fighters are made for this combination and you might even consider giving him the opening for the right cross by dropping your left hand. When he throws the cross, spring the lead front kick/sweep counter. Make sure you judge the distance and the timing right before dropping your left hand. Work this combination on the shield – it is a jolting and morale-sapping counter. (Fig. 59)

Fig. 57

Fig. 58

Fig. 59

Spinning Heel Kick/Spinning Sweep

This is an ambitious combination, but not beyond the reach of a skilled exponent. Timing, power and a strong commitment are necessary.

> **1)** As your opponent throws a rear leg kick (or side or roundhouse kick) withdraw your lead leg. (Fig. 60)

> **2)** As the kick passes you, turn into a spinning heel kick. (Fig. 61)

> **3)** If your opponent ducks to avoid the kick he has settled his weight perfectly for you to launch a fast, strong spinning sweep. (Fig. 62)

This combination calls for good distance and timing appreciation. Make sure that you twist your head, shoulders and hips quickly in both the spinning heel and the spinning sweep so you power through the targets.

Fig. 60

Fig. 61

Fig. 62

Warning: Most rule systems insist on sweeps being at boot height. Any higher and it is a foul.

Transmitting Foot Sweep

The transmitting foot sweep is a technique borrowed from judo and rarely seen in the ring; however, I have used and taught this technique for many years and it is highly effective. It works by adding your sweeping technique to your opponent's own movement and the results can be devastating.

1) As your opponent retreats from you, attack with an orthodox sweeping technique the minute he moves his front foot, but take a line through his lead foot directly into his back foot. (Fig. 63 and Diagram 3)

2) Drive through with plenty of penetration and knock his front foot into his rear foot. (Fig. 64)

3) Continue with the sweep until he topples forward. (Fig. 65)

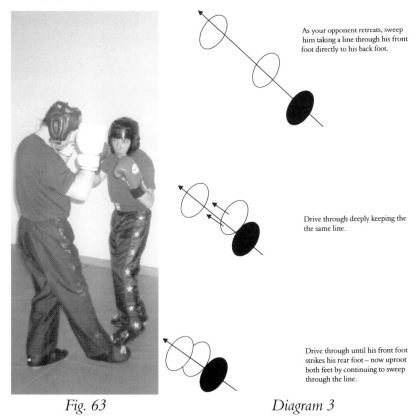

As your opponent retreats, sweep him taking a line through his front foot directly to his back foot.

Drive through deeply keeping the the same line.

Drive through until his front foot strikes his rear foot – now uproot both feet by continuing to sweep through the line.

Fig. 63   *Diagram 3*

Practise this technique slowly by having a partner retreat away from you and synchronise your sweep to add to his movement backwards with his front foot. Once again, timing is all with this, but if you sweep with confidence and speed it is a spectacular throw.

Fig. 64

Fig. 65

Swallow's Turn Sweep

This technique is also taken from judo and, again, it is a subtle and very effective way of dropping your man. Essentially it is a counter to your opponent's sweep.

> **1)** As your opponent performs an orthodox sweep on your front leg, pull back your foot, but do not remove your knee. (Fig. 66)

> **2)** As his foot passes by, snap your foot back and follow his sweeping foot until you connect with it. (Fig. 67)

> **3)** Now with as much hip movement as you can, sweep his attacking foot and down him. (Fig. 68)

Again, timing is crucial, but the single most important detail is not withdrawing the knee as you take your foot out of the path of his sweep. With practice, this is a superb technique that is rarely used and hard to read. Work it until it is second nature.

Fig. 66

Fig. 67

Fig. 68

Roundhouse into Sweep

1) Throw a head-height roundhouse kick at your opponent. (Fig. 69)

2) Instead of pulling your leg back, drive it downwards and throw an orthodox sweep to his lead leg. (Fig. 70)

3) Blast his lead leg away with the flat of your foot, ensuring you carry on through the line of his foot and continue upwards. (Fig. 71)

This technique works by using the momentum of the falling high roundhouse kick and by continuing the arc of the sweep through and upwards so that it falls from his head to the foot and then up like a pendulum.

It works best when your opponent braces himself to block the incoming roundhouse kick, thus trapping his weight and setting it up to be blasted away.

Fig. 69

Fig. 70

Fig. 71

Summary

Sweeps are effective techniques for robbing your opponent of confidence and denying him balance to set up heavy attacks. They also allow you to pin his weight on one leg in order to deliver a telling combination and throw him violently to the floor. Good observation of your opponent's balance is essential.

Timing is the essence of sweeping, and you should always aim to go through the target. The value of power in a sweep should not be underestimated. A strong attack can rip your opponent's legs out from under him even if the timing is not perfect. You should practise power sweeps on a small, light bag set on the floor. Your aim should be to 'launch' the bag. Gradually increase the bag's weight to build up the strength of your sweeps.

Repetition practice is vital if you are to develop the sensitivity, timing and power to gain the maximum from sweeping. Remember: sweeps disrupt, confuse and sap your opponent's morale, as well as set him up for a knockout.

Knockout Combinations

The sport of kick boxing is a severe test of a martial artist's abilities. The different styles and rule systems in force vary from organisation to organisation and range from full contact (kicks above the waist) to Muay Thai. The one common thread of these systems is that you are allowed to hit your opponent with maximum force.

The logical outcome of this is that the kick boxer should aim to stop his opponent in the shortest possible time before he himself is injured. Knocking out your opponent is the fastest way to achieve this. How easy it is to knock him out will depend on a number of things:

1) How forcefully you can hit your opponent.
2) How accurately you can hit him.
3) How durable he is.
4) Correct technique selection.
5) Timing.

Target Selection

Any doctor will tell you that if you hit a person anywhere in the head with sufficient force, you can cause a concussion. Further, any sufficiently strong blow to the body can cause winding, nausea or broken ribs – all of which can put your opponent out of the game. A man who conditions his body well will be able to withstand considerable punishment and may still manage to fight when hurt, especially if he is well motivated.

The ability to take a blow to the head is more problematic. Some people have a 'glass jaw' and will go out like a light when hit; however, providing your opponent doesn't, and has taken the trouble to condition himself and is strongly motivated, he will be hard to stop.

When confronted with such an opponent you need to be aware of the knockout targets, those areas which, when hit, stand the greatest chance of dropping your man for the count. Then it is a question of observing the opportunity and rapidly delivering the correct blow or blows as powerfully as possible.

All the target areas listed here are allowed under *any* of the differing rule systems of kick boxing. It is essential that you are able to see these targets whilst under pressure and deliver powerful blows to them.

The opening up of a knockout target area should be seized upon, but this calls for quick reactions and accurate techniques. All blows to the head create what is known as 'brain shake'. The brain is protected inside the skull by cerebral-spinal fluid. A blow to the head makes the brain move and hit the inside of the skull.

The Five Knockout Targets
(Diagram 4)

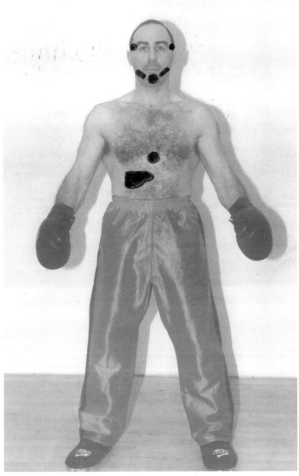

Diagram 4

On the head there are three knockout targets:

1) The jaw: from the point of the chin extending back on both sides for about three inches. This target can be struck horizontally or at a 45-degree angle. Along with its sister target of the point of the chin, the jaw accounts for most knockouts in both kick boxing and boxing.

2) The point of the chin: this can be struck from the side, from underneath or simply straight on. Both the jaw and the chin, when struck, produce rapid 'brain shake' and as such they are the single biggest cause of knockouts.

3) The temple: this is a slightly concave area on the side of the head in line with the eye. The concave surface acts to concentrate the force of the blow.

On the body there are two knockout targets:

1) The liver: this lies half under and half below the floating ribs on the right-hand side of the body. Getting hit here is akin to being kicked in the groin. A rule of thumb guide to its location is to think of it lying directly beneath the elbow when your opponent is in full guard. Strike it straight in or upwards at 45 degrees.

2) The solar plexus: this area is directly below the sternum. Striking here causes the diaphragm to spasm, preventing the lungs from expanding and so winding your opponent. Strike it straight in or upward.

In theory, any blow to these targets will produce the goods, but some techniques allow a cleaner, more accurate application of force to the target. This is borne out by observation of countless knockouts and stoppages. It is a question of using the best tool to do the job. Further, delivering combinations that strike more than one of these areas will significantly increase your chances of a clean knockout, for example, a left shovel hook to the liver followed by a left hook to the jaw.

Married to this is that subtlest of arts – timing. Small errors are frequently the start of a disaster. If you can create a weakness in your opponent's guard through the use of movement and feints, then you can launch a killer combination that zeros in on the knockout targets. Counter-attacks flow from your opponent's errors and it is no surprise to learn that many counter-attacks lead to knockouts.

Unforced errors in your opponent's technique may reveal a knockout opportunity, such as failing to return his jabbing hand to the guard after attempting to strike you or letting his arms go wide as he kicks.

The skilled fighter should be observant, quick to react and ruthless in execution whenever an opportunity presents itself.

Close-Range Knockouts

Kill the body and the head will die! This is an old boxing maxim that has a lot going for it. In essence it means that if you hit the body hard, your opponent will drop his guard to protect his body and thereby leave his head exposed.

The Three-Punch Kill: shovel hook – hook – cross

Targets: liver – jaw – jaw

When your opponent moves his rear elbow, either through an error in his guard or during the execution of a technique, you should:

> **1)** Throw a powerful shovel hook to his liver (he will immediately drop his elbow to prevent you throwing another. If he doesn't, hit it again! (Fig. 72)
>
> **2)** Next throw a tight left hook to his jaw (or temple). (Fig. 73)
>
> **3)** Finish the knockout combination by throwing a committed cross to the jaw on the other side of his face. (Fig. 74)

Practise this combination on the focus pads, remembering to curve your body behind the hooks and to take half a pace forward with your rear foot during the execution of the cross.

If your opponent has a tendency to overreact when you throw head punches, you can turn this combination into a medium-range attack by preceding it with a jab/cross. This five-punch combination is fast and very strong; practise it on the focus pads and be sure to curve your body behind the shots. Thrown with commitment this combination is the perfect way to close off a fight.

Fig. 72

Fig. 73

Fig. 74

Prising Open the Guard: uppercut – hook – spinning backfist

Targets: point of the chin – jaw – temple

Although most fighters at some time in a fight allow their guard to widen or drop, there are fighters with very good discipline who are particularly adept at staying tight.

Hitting the target areas on such fighters is difficult. An opponent with a tight guard must be lured or pressured into loosening that guard. For the moment though we will deal with when your opponent has allowed gaps to be created in a full guard, and outline some tactics for opening up tight guards.

1) When your opponent's guard opens through the middle, throw an uppercut between his gloves and on to the point of his chin. (Fig. 75)
2) Pivot strongly over your lead foot and throw a tight left hook to his jaw. (Fig. 76)
3) Finish him with a fast spinning backfist to the temple. (Fig. 77)

Fig. 75

Fig. 76

Fig. 77

The uppercut/hook section of this combination requires you to pivot strongly and curve your body behind the shots. The spinning backfist requires a rapid spin, keeping your striking fist tight to your body until the last instant, making the pay-off extremely hard to see.

If your opponent has a tight guard the simplest and most obvious way to prise it open is to throw a feint lead hook to the side of your opponent's head. When he shifts his guard to cover the attack, pop the uppercut onto his chin and continue with a lead hook to the jaw and then go straight into the spinning backfist. This ruse will fool a novice or a nervous fighter, but an experienced man is harder to hoodwink.

None of us like getting hit, so the feint hook – uppercut – hook – spinning backfist combination works best on the experienced man after you have caught him with a one-off well-timed left hook. For now he is – albeit temporarily – conditioned to react.

Whether he likes it or not, your opponent will find himself reacting to another hook by overemphasising his guard and allowing the rear hand to drift out to cover your feint hook. When this occurs, go straight into the uppercut – hook – spinning backfist combination.

Practise this on the focus pads. Have your partner hold the pads close to his chest and lean towards you. Then he should snap up the pads without warning. Launch the three-blow combination as soon as you see the target opening up.

Medium-Range Knockouts

At this distance all techniques can be applied. It is very dangerous to loiter in medium range; however, it is the perfect range at which to finish your opponent because there is enough space to bring every technique online.

The Man-Stopper: snapping front kick – cross – hook

Targets: liver – point of the chin – jaw

This combination is fast, simple and powerful. I strongly recommend that you commit to the kick and let the punches fly! When your opponent raises his guard (particularly after overreacting to a head shot or a feint head shot) unleash the combination.

1) Throw a snapping lead leg front kick to his liver. (Fig. 78)
2) Throw a committed cross to the point of his chin. (Fig. 79)
3) Now pivot fast over your lead foot and deliver a strong lead hook to his jaw. (Fig. 80)

Fig. 78

Fig. 79

There are lots of opportunities to throw this combination, but in essence it comes down to whenever your opponent, for any reason, raises his guard and exposes his body to attack. The kick will wind your opponent and force him to drop his guard, exposing his head.

Fig. 80

It should also be borne in mind that the second and final parts of the combination can also be achieved by driving in with a strong body kick when his guard is tightly defending the body (to 'anchor' his guard down low), then letting the cross/hook finish smash home.

Go with the Flow: hook – spinning backfist – backthrust kick
Targets: jaw – temple – solar plexus
This combination uses circular power and is, as a result, extremely powerful. The backthrust kick is hidden by the spinning backfist and can be thrown with maximum finishing power.

> **1)** When your opponent drops his rear hand, throw a medium-range lead hook to the jaw. (Fig. 81)

> **2)** Continue turning and throw a right spinning backfist to the temple. (Fig. 82)

> **3)** Drive the backthrust kick into your opponent's solar plexus. (Fig. 83)

Fig. 81

Fig. 82

Fig. 83

It is not necessary to completely straighten the leg when the backthrust kick is thrown at medium range. The spin puts the power into the kick, and kicking with a bent leg is a very effective way of delivering it.

The opportunities for delivering the hook that starts this knockout combination are numerous. I have listed some of the more common ones below.

1) When your opponent allows his rear guarding hand to go slightly backwards when throwing a jab. This is called scissoring and is a common error in novices and experienced fighters alike.

2) When he fails to keep his rear guarding hand high enough, either through fatigue or lack of concentration

3) When he fails to return the rear hand to the guard after delivering a cross. A frequent cause of this error is when your opponent is 'gun happy' – that is, more intent on hitting you than guarding himself.

4) When he fails to keep his chin down whilst executing techniques – a failure to observe correct form.

You should pounce on your opponent the instant you see the rear guarding hand move out of position. Anticipation, quick reactions and the ability to deliver power accurately will see this combination achieve the maximum effect.

Long-Range Knockouts

This is the hardest range from which to launch a knockout and for the most obvious of reasons – distance. The longer it takes your knockout technique or combination to arrive, the more time your opponent has to see and react to it, and therefore the less chance it has of getting home cleanly.

Long-range knockouts are opportunistic by nature and require great accuracy. It is the area where the specialist kicker comes into his own. A paradox exists here: we have already said that launching an attack at long range takes more time, but it is also true that you can score a clean knockout because your opponent will not expect an attack launched at such range!

Strongest Blow, Weakest Target: spinning backthrust kick – cross
Target areas: liver – point of the chin

This combination is lethal. In the previous medium-range combination we saw a backthrust kick used as a finishing technique. Here we will show how it can be used as an opportunistic opener at long range.

Of all the techniques in the kick boxer's arsenal, the spinning backthrust kick is arguably the most powerful. Although it may be thrown to the head, without doubt the body offers a safer and larger target.

For the experienced fighter with good control of technique and good timing, it is possible to deliver the backthrust kick to the most sensitive of targets – the liver. When the strongest of blows hits the weakest of targets, there can only be one result: knockout.

We have already said that the position of your opponent's rear guarding elbow is crucial when locating the liver. It stands to reason that if your opponent is throwing a cross then his liver will be exposed to attack.

The experienced fighter can try a variety of ways to get his opponent to throw the cross. One inducement is by dropping his own lead guarding hand.

1) The instant your opponent throws a cross to your exposed head, spin and drive a hard spinning backthrust kick to his liver. (Fig. 84)

2) Continue to spin and deliver a hard (left) cross to the point of the chin. (Fig. 85)

Another chance to throw this combination is when your opponent is moving back rapidly under pressure and has allowed his guard to widen. Throw a feint jab to concentrate his mind on his upper body, then launch the combination.

Fig. 84

Fig. 85

Win with the Spin: spinning hook kick – spinning front kick

Target areas: jaw/temple – liver

As stated before, long-range knockouts are opportunistic by nature. Your opponent presents ambush opportunities either when he relaxes his guard or during the execution of a technique.

Close observation of his habits and tendencies in the opening rounds of a fight may point to such an opportunity. In this case, it is when he allows the rear guarding hand to drop position to expose the right side of the jaw and right temple.

> **1)** As soon as this occurs, spin rapidly and strike him with a spinning hook kick to either the jaw or the temple. (Fig. 86)

> **2)** Continue with the spin and throw a snappy front kick to his liver. (Fig. 87)

Timing is vital with this combination, as is good technique. If you are not a specialist kicker you have no business throwing this combination – and if you have to stop to think whether you are a specialist kicker, then you're not!

Two tools are needed to develop the kicks essential for long-range knockouts. First, the big bag to build power and secondly, the focus pads, to build accuracy. Many hours must be given over to developing fast reactions and kicks that can be used the instant an opportunity presents itself.

Fig. 86

Fig. 87

Summary

Any fighter with power can effect a knockout, but the experienced man with superior timing and craft, deliberately aiming for the knockout targets, can turn a chance into a near certainty.

A fighter aiming to be a champion should study the knockout closely. Speed, power, timing and target recognition will turn a scoring combination into the finish of the fight.

The instant your opponent shows that he is hurt, confused or hesitant you should unleash a killer combination or set of combinations and finish him.

The techniques and combinations above are not meant to comprise an exhaustive list. To obtain the most value from this information, examine your own preferred or most commonly used techniques, and think of how best to apply them against the five listed targets areas. Do it, and do it first; if you don't – he will.

Close-Range Fighting

Fighting at close range is an indispensable skill. If you are to win consistently, you must attain a full appreciation of its requirements, because whatever type of fighter you are or whatever range you prefer to fight at, you will, at some stage in a fight, be *compelled* to work at close range.

This is particularly true if one fighter gains ascendancy during the fight, for he will try to bring the fight to a finish by moving in and hammering home the final blows. Equally, if under pressure yourself, you will be forced back into a corner or onto the ropes and have to fight from there. In either case you will end up at close range.

All skills – blocking, parrying, slipping, ducking, laying back, punching, sweeping and even kicking – can be used close in, but note that the dynamics of speed and power change. To that extent, close-range fighting can be considered a mini-fighting system in itself.

This mini-fighting system has ground rules that have to be appreciated by the fighter aspiring to the top, for at no time must you forget that close range is the most dangerous range of all and mastery of it is the winning factor.

The Ground Rules

1) First protect yourself. Whatever factors are involved at close range, you are inside the ultimate knockout range and to loiter is to risk getting severely worked over.

2) Balance. Your opponent will try to push you off-balance and hit you as you adjust. Therefore you must build a repertoire of balance-shifting manoeuvres that help you retain your balance and dislodge his in turn.

3) Power. The dynamics of power change at close range, requiring body shifting rather than long limb movements to obtain power and leverage.

4) Speed. Reflex speed is the primary element, followed by limb speed. If you are slow at close range you are dead in the water.

5) Mirroring. Synchronise your technique with your opponent's, so that his attempt to hit you is defeated by slotting an attack into the gap left in his defence.

These ground rules, or to put it another way, these areas of skill, must be mastered if you are to survive and win.

First Protect Yourself

At close range, rapid changes in stance and guard are essential to keep the initiative. Stance and guard must always be fluid creations if you are to function at your maximum potential.

Many fighters never change guard whatever the range, and their only solution to close-range fighting is to tighten the one that they favour. This is a mistake that could cost them the fight.

We will examine the stances and guards that must be mastered. It cannot be emphasised too much that you must experiment in training to gain a fuller understanding of the principles outlined below.

The Full Guard

The full guard (Fig. 88) is not recommended as a first choice when fighting at close range. It is too open and allows your opponent too many options when attacking you, particularly with angled shovel hooks to the body, uppercuts through the middle, body hooks below the elbows and short front kicks off the lead leg. That said, if you have weakened your opponent and are closing in for the kill, then the full guard allows you the maximum options for attack.

Fig. 88

The Half Guard

The half guard (Fig. 89) allows you to shut off most target areas from attack, especially if your opponent is also in a half guard – that way you fit together like two triangular shapes. (Diagram 5) This changes when your opponent is a southpaw.

Fig. 89

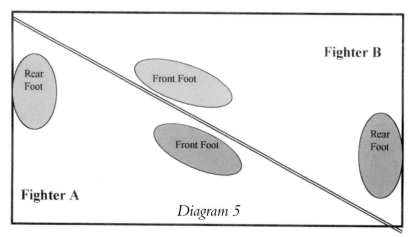

Diagram 5

Fig. 90

From the half guard you can make use of a tight lead hook to the head or the body (Fig. 90), and a short cross thrown directly across your own chest. (Fig. 91)

Sweeping your opponent's lead leg is also a possibility and can cause the disruption of his guard. (Fig. 92) Should this occur, attack immediately with a strong combination.

Fig. 91

Fig. 92

The Cross Guard

The cross guard (Fig. 93) prevents your opponent from scoring cleanly. It confines his blows to the edges of the target area and makes him work hard to score. When you add a bobbing up and down motion you can move forward putting him under tremendous pressure whilst giving you the opportunity to throw punishing hooks to both the head and the body.

If you are trapped in a corner or on the ropes, this guard combined with movement can also work defensively, offering the best option for survival.

Fig. 93

Experiment with full guard, half guard and cross guard. Look to hit around the edges of your opponent's guard and when he spreads his elbows to cover this, switch to shovel hooks (Fig. 94), uppercuts (Fig. 95) and lead leg front kicks through the middle. (Fig. 96)

When he adjusts by tightening up his guard, switch back to hooks around the edges. Your task is to take the initiative and keep it.

Fig. 94

A good jack-in-the-box technique at close range is a tight spinning backthrust kick. (Fig. 97) Keep close to your opponent and then turn away quickly, driving your heel into his liver. Because of the turn, you do not need to straighten your leg to get power.

Structured sparring is the preferred practice method for stance and guard training. You should practise by placing yourself in a corner or on the ropes and have a partner hit you at half speed and half power. (Figs. 98 to 100)

Fig. 95

You should change guard continually whilst moving your upper body to frustrate his attempts to score cleanly. Next, reverse the roles and try

Fig. 96

Fig. 97

to break down your opponent's guard by intelligent use of combinations. Always seek to get him to move his guard, then drive a shot into the gap you have created.

The variations on this theme are endless and should form a good basis for your own experimentation. A simple aid to constructing penetrating combinations is 'straight and round, body and head, hand and leg'.

Fig. 98

Fig. 99

Fig. 100

Balance

For a fighter, balance is a constant preoccupation. If your balance is dislodged you are extremely vulnerable. A stronger, more aggressive fighter will frequently try to back you into a corner or onto the ropes where he will aim to destroy you with heavy shots.

Simply pushing back against a stronger opponent is tiring and doomed to fail. You must prevent him backing you up by practising body-shifting manoeuvres that turn the tables and leave him vulnerable to your attack. Effective tactics are:

1) Yielding to pressure.

2) Breaking his balance.

3) Stealing the punch.

4) The lay-on.

Yielding to Pressure

When your opponent pushes you backwards, pivot away from the line of force. This will cause him to go past you. Now strike him from the other side with a hook. (Fig. 101) The more force he applies, the better this works. Yield quickly and time the hook for maximum effect.

Fig. 101

Breaking his Balance

When pushing, your opponent must set his feet. The axis of his stance is an imaginary line running through each foot. His stance is strong when his feet are in line with the direction of his pushing and conversely, extremely weak when you push at right angles to this axis – the line of force. (Diagram 6)

In order to break his balance, rapidly pivot away from the direction of his force, then push with your shoulder at right angles to the axis of his stance. (Fig. 102)

Warning: you can push with your body, but blatant pushing with your hands will attract penalties, perhaps even a disqualification. Be subtle!

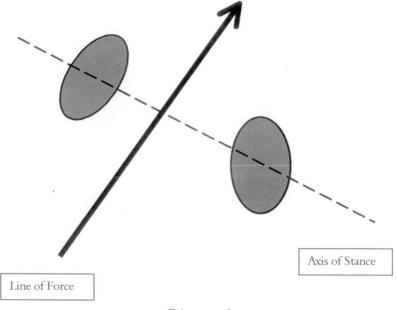

Axis of Stance

Line of Force

Diagram 6

Fig. 102

Stealing the Punch

Stealing the punch is a deft way of applying a short cross. When you and your opponent are pushing together, suddenly withdraw your lead shoulder enough to drive a short cross to his chin. Now quickly close the gap by pushing your shoulder forward again. (Fig. 103)

Fig. 103

The Lay-On

Another tactic that works is to simply lay on your opponent. Instead of pushing back and expending energy, place your weight on him and make him burn up precious energy by keeping you off. (Fig. 104) This is a subtle art and with practice you can learn to time the lay-on in order to frustrate him. Experiment!

Fig. 104

Power

The dynamics of power change at close range. You don't have the luxury of building up limb speed, and therefore power, over a distance.

To attain power in your techniques, you must rapidly pivot your feet, hips and shoulders. Correct body alignment together with this rapid pivoting will produce knockout power. To train for this you must spend time on the big bag – the biggest you can find.

Lean against the bag and push it off-centre. This will feel like the weight of your opponent. Now, without moving back, pivot and hit the bag forcefully. (Fig. 105)

At first it will feel cramped and awkward, but the more you practise, the more natural it begins to feel and the more power you will attain. Spending time on this drill will be well rewarded.

Fig. 105   *Fig. 105a*

Speed

Speed at close range is highly dependent on quick reactions. There are three elements to true speed:

1) Limb speed: fast hands and feet that can deliver an attack or defence once in position.

2) Body speed: fast footwork that carries your body into range in order to launch the limb.

3) Reflex speed: reaction to a stimulus that delivers the correct skill in response to an attack (that is, a defence or counter) or initiates an attack of your own on presentation of an opportunity.

Reflex speed is the most important element when fighting at close range. Limb speed will also play a part, but body speed – fast footwork – is virtually redundant for the simple reason that you are already in range.

To train your reflex speed, you must use the focus pads. Have a partner crouch over at close range, holding the pads close to his chest. Your partner snaps up the pads whilst you launch a technique or combination as soon as you see the target. (Fig. 106)

Fig. 106

Mirroring

Mirroring is a tactic that speeds up your responses. It requires you to stand in front of a mirror throwing techniques and noting where you are open to a counter-attack. Wherever you are open, your opponent will be.

It is a system in which your opponent's attack selects your counter. Essential to this is the concept of recognition-primed decision, which in turn is linked to visualisation.

Recognition-primed decision is when you unleash a power attack or counter the instant you perceive an opportunity. You see it, recognise it and take him out. This is reaction born of hours of practice in the gym and – more importantly – hours in the fighting ring.

Mirroring requires fast reactions, a good range of techniques and the ability to stay in close and survive. Its use is suggested only for someone with a high level of training.

To practise mirroring, stand in front of a mirror and throw a jab. Now observe what part of your target area is open to attack whilst you are jabbing. What you see in the mirror is what you see when an opponent is attacking you. Where you are open, he will be open too.

Now throw a selection of techniques – cross/uppercut/front kick/roundhouse kick and so on, until you have a complete picture of all target areas that come online as a result of throwing those techniques.

The next phase is to work out selected counters that will best strike the exposed target area. For instance, when your opponent jabs, his leading side ribs become exposed; therefore consider using a lead front kick, a cross to the body or a lead side kick.

The greater your repertoire, the greater choice of counters you have. The would-be champion always looks to expand his technical responses.

It is at close range that we see mirroring's true value. For example, as your opponent throws a lead hook to the head, duck and counter with a hook to the body. (Fig. 107)

Alternatively, as your opponent throws a short cross to the head, counter with a lead front kick to the body. (Fig. 108)

By careful observation in front of a mirror and the acquisition of a solid range of counter techniques, you can heavily punish a fighter at close range.

Fig. 107

Fig. 108

Summary

The ground rules are true for everybody. Be aware of those areas of skill that you must acquire. Give time over to practising at close range and train with a variety of opponents – tall, short, strong, southpaw and so on. Experiment!

Effective close-range fighting is an essential area of skill for the would-be champion. Master it or be the victim of it!

At medium range all weapons can be brought to bear. Timing and distance appreciation have to be at their best. Medium range is the transitory distance that must be crossed in both directions, with maximum speed.

Correct mastery of distance is essential if you are to control the fight. As a rule of thumb, you should be on the inside fighting, the outside circling, or crossing medium range en route to an attack or retreating into long range. Never, ever loiter in medium range.

Long range offers the greatest safety, but reduced chances to attack. We have said already that long range is where the kicker comes into his own, but it is also the place to retreat to when you are not actually launching an attack. It is also the range for reconnaissance in the opening rounds of a fight.

Part Two: Tactics and Ringcraft

'The best fighters are Chameleons.'

Tactics and ringcraft are arts. They are the application of the particular ways of attacking and defending that yield the best from your techniques.

Here I will make a controversial statement – you do not have to be the best *fighter* in the ring to win a contest, only the best *performer*.

It is a question of using the tactics that place you in a superior position to that of your opponent and forcing him to fight in ways that place him at a disadvantage – bringing your sharpest edge against his weakest side.

Naturally, your opponent will be trying to do this to you as well, and the man who applies himself the best will win. For you to do this, you have to understand what type of fighter you are. There are five basic types of fighter or, to put it another way, five fighting styles.

The Five Types of Fighters

1) The Thief: this is a hit-and-run fighter. A man that scores and moves, never standing still, never letting you rest. He is frequently misunderstood and described as a defensive fighter. This is a flawed analysis, for the Thief always looks to score. Expect him to be a master of timing and mobility for this is his chief means of survival and victory. A Thief thrives in a large ring.

Example: Dylan Spencer in his classy victory over Michel Al Tali for the WKMA European Championship in 1999. Al Tali was a typical Killer with a record of 25 fights/23 wins/18 of them by knockout. Dylan never let him get set and scored freely throughout the contest. Al Tali nearly burst a blood vessel with frustration.

2) The Killer: this is a trap-and-kill fighter. His whole game plan is to back you onto the ropes or into a corner and break you up. Usually, but not exclusively, he is a puncher, and a body puncher at that. In the opening phases of a fight the Killer will sometimes stalk in order to weigh up the opposition before pouncing.

The Killer too is, more often that not, misunderstood. He is thought to be just a banger, but in reality he reduces fighting to its most simple yet most subtle – finding your man and finishing him. Expect him to fight at close range where he is at his most destructive. The Killer thrives in a small ring and is very aware of the additional pressure this creates for his opponent.

Example: Mark Walters in his war with Eval Denton in 1995 for the K.I.C.K. British Championship. Mark continually pushed Eval on to the back foot and hammered in vicious body punches. Eval is also a Killer, but on this occasion he was outworked by Mark, who showed true desire.

3) The Ambusher: this is a counter-fighter. He manoeuvres to entice you into an ill-timed or poorly thought-out attack, and then he pounces, beating you to the punch and scoring with a heavy combination. His aim is to catch you just at the moment of moving in, thereby doubling up his striking power.

I believe a cool-headed, heavy-hitting Ambusher is the most dangerous opponent a fighter can face. Expect him to be a master of timing and distance with hair-trigger reactions.

All fighters throw counters, but the Ambusher is a master of drawing his opponent out and making him fight at the wrong moment and the wrong range.

Example: Tim Izzli in his well-crafted victory over Bayran Kolok for the European Title in 1990. Tim waited, watched and countered the heavy-kicking Kolok time and time again. It was nothing short of a masterclass for the spectators.

4) The Raider: this is a fighter who measures his attacks and applies increasingly greater pressure with longer and harder combinations until you are worn down, ready for the final raid – the kill. His attacks can be likened to progressively heavier weights being applied to your chest. Expect him to use heavy kicks and punches to the body.

The nature of raiding means that the Raider picks up vital intelligence on his opponent before committing to a heavy or sustained attack. By this means he is able to increase his chances of survival and victory.

Example: Garnet 'Chill' John in his electric victory over Chris Long in 1999. This was a superb fight in which Garnet applied tremendous and increasing pressure on the game and skilful Chris Long. Garnet went on to win a version of the world title shortly after this.

5) The Southpaw: in the context of this book, this is a fighter who is not by birth left-handed, but who has deliberately chosen to fight with his right side forward.

By choosing to fight in this way he puts his natural/ stronger side in front, thus giving him fast and powerful leading shots with both the lead hand and foot.

It also throws out his opponent's timing and distance, causing hesitations in his attack and defence. Expect the Southpaw to have strong and penetrating opening attacks and good distance appreciation. (For a more complete analysis of the Southpaw see *Kick Boxing – A Framework for Success*, Chapter Six.)

Clash of Styles

When you are confronted by a style of fighter that you recognise, you must immediately apply the tactics that will win. Below are some examples of how one fighter imposes his own style on the opposition.

1) Killer versus Thief: use diagonal movement – first left, then right, then left – to back him against the ropes or into a corner. Plant fear in his mind and keep it there. In the opening rounds of a fight, a Killer will seek to hit the Thief with a series of punishing body shots to weaken him and rob him of the stamina he needs to continually move. At the first sign of weakness the Killer should pounce and bring the fight to an explosive conclusion.

2) Thief versus Killer: a Killer needs to plant his feet in order to unload. Sweep him to deny him the firm base he needs and rattle in sharp stop-hit jabs and front kicks to disturb his attempts to come close. Sharp, stinging blows and combinations should be used to frustrate the Killer and make him reckless. If he grows impatient and lunges in, meet him with a sharp combination and then move off. Hit – run – hit – run should be the litany in the Thief's head.

3) Raider versus Southpaw: circle to your left away from his rear hand and foot. This brings your own rear (strongest) hand and foot online. Dig him hard and often. Once in position, never let him rest. Raid him using sudden, seemingly random attacks so that he cannot settle into his rhythm. Use heavy right-hand punches and kicks to rattle him.

4) Southpaw versus Ambusher: use lots of feints and distractions to draw the counter, then pepper him as he commits to his counter-attack. Watch his face for any signs of hesitation or confusion – then whack him hard!

Study Chart One below and think through the tactics that would win each particular match.

Thief	versus	Thief
Killer	versus	Killer
Ambusher	versus	Ambusher
Raider	versus	Raider
Southpaw	versus	Southpaw
Thief	versus	Killer
Killer	versus	Ambusher
Ambusher	versus	Raider
Raider	versus	Southpaw
Southpaw	versus	Thief
Thief	versus	Ambusher
Killer	versus	Raider
Ambusher	versus	Southpaw
Raider	versus	Thief
Southpaw	versus	Killer
Thief	versus	Raider
Killer	versus	Southpaw
Southpaw	versus	Ambusher
Thief	versus	Southpaw

Chart One

Remember that the chart illustrates only the possibilities thrown up by the five basic types of fighter meeting each other. Review the chart again and ask yourself which tactics you would personally employ in each case given your current fighting type and skill level, and then ask yourself what additional skills you might need to achieve success against each different type of fighter. The analysis will enable you to work out the problems that could confront you in a future fight.

Choosing a Fighting Style

Many fighters never give active consideration to what type of fighter they are or should be. They 'just do it', or they find that their physique predisposes them to becoming a particular type of fighter and they settle for that, becoming the best they can within that style. This is too haphazard for the man aiming at the top.

The man setting out to be a world champion must be aware of the advantages of developing differing fighting styles and the combinations of types that are both logical and profitable. If you are in the sport with the aim of reaching the top, you owe it to yourself to consider the options.

Although there are only five basic types of fighter, many fighters have the ability to master more than one style. They may in fact change styles several times within a contest, starting out in the early stages as a Thief, then turning into a Raider to apply increasing pressure before changing again, this time into a Killer, to trap and kill the opponent in the final stages.

Certain types marry particularly well with others to create very effective fighting styles. A fighter who blends differing types of fighting styles is called a Hybrid. Many fighters are, to a greater or lesser extent, Hybrids, even if they are not aware of it. Generally the particular blend of styles is logical, for example, Southpaw-Thief.

Below are some examples of Hybrids together with suggested tactics for dealing with them. Once again, you should consider what responses you would have to make given your present fighting style and the options it provides you with.

Tactics against Hybrids

Thief-Ambusher: a very dangerous Hybrid fighter who hits and runs away only to ambush you, should you be lured into pursuing him. The way to deal with this type of opponent is to hurt him early and keep him in trouble. Never allow him to regain the initiative.

Southpaw-Thief: an extremely slippery Hybrid who will pose no end of problems with regard to distance and timing. My own instructor Geoff Britton was just such a fighter and he caused me, and everyone else, nightmares when trying to catch him. The only way to deal with this type of opponent is continual pressure – never let him rest.

Killer-Raider: the ultimate pressure Hybrid. He will pressurise you until you have nowhere to go, and then cut you off and kill you. A strong, fit Killer-Raider with a sound chin is a nightmare to deal with. Your best defence is to be a highly mobile Thief. Trevor Ambrose was a master Thief with the ability to give weight away, relying on his superb timing and mobility skills. His fight against the powerful Winston Walker was a classic Thief versus Killer-Raider encounter, and one of the most fascinating fights that I have ever seen. The fight went right down to the wire and we only knew that Trevor Ambrose had won when the last bell sounded. Both men had provided a masterclass.

Southpaw-Raider: a very frustrating and painful Hybrid who will be slippery when it suits him and hit you in sustained bursts when your frustration shows. The way to deal with this Hybrid is to trap and kill when he is passive, and hit and run when he is active.

Southpaw-Thief-Ambusher: unless you are very skilful, fighting this Hybrid will mean total pain. Consider for a moment the tactical switches that would be necessary to deal with him. Ironically, the solution is not to go more technical, but to reduce your style to the most basic – Killer. Trap him and pound him, never allowing his timing and mobility skills to function at their best.

By becoming a Hybrid you will dramatically improve your chances of gaining a significant title. However, there is one more type of fighter. A master of styles – the Chameleon.

Chameleons

Chameleons can change types according to who is in front of them to prevent their opponents scoring freely whilst maximising their own chances of victory.

They have the ability to transform themselves from a dancing, evasive Thief into a heavy-clubbing Killer; from a master Ambusher to a persistent Raider before switching sides to become a Southpaw. There can be no doubt – Chameleons are the best technical fighters around. Fortunately, they are very, very rare.

A Chameleon may change for the whole duration of a fight or change several times within a fight, perhaps inside a round, in order to constantly outwit and outperform the opposition.

Chameleons are mentally agile, technically fluent and bear the mark of greatness. Just to clarify matters, a Chameleon is a master fighter capable of switching styles at will to suit the circumstances confronting him, whereas a Hybrid is a fighter who chooses to mix a number of types without necessarily changing that mix every time he confronts someone new.

I realise that you cannot change the type of fighter you are overnight, and further, you may not want to, but be sure of one thing – if you are aiming for the top you are limiting your options with this attitude.

If it is at all within your grasp you should try to become a Chameleon or at least a versatile Hybrid. The advantages gained are precisely what you need to set yourself apart from the herd.

Summary

You will probably have a basic style and be one of the five basic types when you start fighting; however, different opponents require different solutions, so it is important to have more than one style at your disposal as you progress through the rankings. Ultimately, you should aim to become a Chameleon, although this will take considerable training and will on your part.

At the very least you should add further styles to your repertoire and become a Hybrid of two or more of the basic types. This is part of what I meant in the introduction when I said that to be a champion you have to make space in your life in order to grow, to become something other than just another fighter.

So although you may be inclined naturally in one direction or another, you must seek to make choices that suit the requirements for victory. A plan to use a particular tactic or combination of tactics in order to bring about a certain aim is called strategy.

Part Three: The Game Plan

'Failing to prepare is preparing to fail.'

In Part Two we looked at the different types of fighter and what tactics they are likely to employ. In Part Three we go beyond that and look at why and how the intelligent fighter should take control of the contest.

The Generic Game Plan

First off, it has to be said that whatever you try to do to your opponent, his task is to stop you – quite literally! If your opponent is unknown to you, then a fight potentially becomes very dangerous.

To prevent yourself walking blindly into disaster, the would-be champion has to impose structure on the fight from the beginning to the end. To achieve this, you must divide the fight into three sections: the recce; dominating the fight; and the endgame.

The Recce

The recce is an intelligence-gathering exercise carried out in the opening quarter of a fight. It enables you to build up a picture of your opponent's potential to damage you and your opportunities to damage him. To this end, there are five areas that you should investigate:

1) Guard/stance
- Where are the openings?
- Does he drop his right or left hand whilst in guard?
- Does he return to a tight guard after hitting or does his guard spread due to concentrating too hard on hitting (tunnel vision)?
- Do his elbows drift out from his body?
- When he kicks, do his arms spread for balance?
- How does he stand?
- What is the best way to sweep him?
- Does fatigue or pain cause his guard to alter?

2) Openings
- Is there a pattern to the way he attacks?
- Does he lead with hands or legs?
- Is it always the same opening – that is, a jab or a front leg technique?
- Does he use feints before he commits himself with a strong attack?
- Does he time his openings or does he lunge and hope?
- Does he telegraph his intent?

3) Technique
• Are his choices sound?
• Does he use some techniques repeatedly regardless of their effect?
• Does he throw techniques 'cold' – that is, without timing or distance appreciation?
• Does he use inappropriate techniques such as high, flashy kicks where a solid jab would get the job done?
• Does he use techniques singularly or in combinations?
• Does he vary the angles on his techniques or is he one-dimensional?

4) Style
• Is he one of the five types of fighter?
• Does he always fight the same way or is he able to change according to the circumstances (Chameleon)?
• Does he combine various types of fighting (Hybrid)?
• What is his preferred distance – short, medium or long range?
• Is he a legs man or a hands man?
• Does he trade on durability and walk through your techniques?

5) Qualities
• What are his recurring strengths and weaknesses?
• Does he possess knockout power?
• Can he take a punch?
• Does he gain or lose confidence when under pressure?
• Is he fit or out of shape?
• Does he learn quickly or does he fail to respond effectively to being hit?

This is a basic checklist that should form part of your recce. It is not exhaustive. Bear in mind that you must do more than just look. You should test him and learn; use the jab and lead leg front kick as they are fast and do not overcommit you. An effective recce observes, calculates, retests and reaffirms.

You should finish the recce with as full a picture of your opponent's potential as possible. Never assume that you have the entire picture, and continue to observe and adapt according to what your opponent presents throughout the fight.

It should be remembered that your opponent will be conducting his own recce, so you should not parade all your skills. Throw in the odd dummy, for instance, throw some heavy kicks if you are a puncher or some heavy punches if you are a kicker. Be careful not to show your natural rhythm and preferred distance in the opening rounds. Learn about him and prevent him from learning about you.

Dominating the Fight

The next phase is all about applying the knowledge gained during the recce and using it to dominate the fight. Ideally, you will select the correct style, correct techniques, and correct distance and timing to seize control of the fight.

The idea is to get in front and stay there. Your opponent should be constantly employed in trying to 'solve' you. By initiating the tactics, you get to choose where and when to fight.

This phase normally takes up the middle two quarters of a fight. Naturally, you will bring the fight to a close as soon as possible, but for now I want you to hold on to the concept of gathering intelligence and applying the lessons learned.

A very essential part of dominating the fight is weakening your opponent. This is achieved (particularly in long-distance fights) by the use of solid body shots with kicks and punches to erode his fighting capability. There are two effects from this. Firstly, you rob him of his stamina and therefore his ability to fight to his full potential. Secondly, you cause him pain and discomfort that deters him from 'opening up', reducing his ability to fight effectively.

Nothing deters a fighter more than hard, debilitating body shots. Visit his liver, floating ribs and solar plexus often.

Deception

Deception is another way of controlling your opponent. If he cannot read you or analyse your techniques and tactics, he will be constantly behind the game, leaving him guessing and making mistakes.

If you are able to disguise your intentions he is forced to react rather than take control. Deception can be something as simple as a hand feint prior to throwing a punch, or as complex as an entire game plan for the fight. Deception can be used in technique, tactics or strategy.

1) Deception in Technique

• Change the angles of techniques frequently to throw out his defences. Find ways of altering how you stand: drop and blast punches upwards; raise up and blast down; step to the side and fire kicks into him; find the gaps in his guard and exploit them.

• Change the timing of techniques by varying the speed and using feints judiciously.

• Change the distance at which you throw certain techniques. Find ways to throw kicks from close in and punches from far out. Play with this concept and experiment in the gym before taking it into the ring.

2) Deception in Tactics

• Alter your fighting style to confuse your opponent and make him hesitate to commit to attacks and counter-attacks.

• When he wants to be active, go passive. When he wants to be passive, go active. Randomness is the key here. Use it to prevent him settling into the fight.

3) Deception in Strategy

• This is the advanced game plan that you create as the means to victory. You can add elements of randomness and deception.

The Endgame

The last quarter of a fight is where a contest is won or lost. Just because you have weighed him up and worked him over doesn't mean that he is out of the game.

His corner men will now be impressing on him that he is behind and needs to drastically change the flow of play. They will be concentrating his mind on those techniques that have been most successful for him so far. They will be reminding him of his friends and relatives who are watching. In short, he will enter this quarter as a man on a mission, and the mission is you!

You have important choices to make in this last and crucial quarter.

- Do you go for a knockout and finish on a high?

- Do you settle for accurate point-scoring coupled with remaining elusive?

- Do you increase the power, tempo or speed to make him crack open?

- Do you bring out your speciality to surprise and dismay him?

The final quarter of a fight is the perfect time to throw that little bit of magic that you've been saving. This is the perfect moment for a flying kick or morale-busting sweep.

Chart Two is a schematic representation of a generic game plan, setting out options and potentially successful methods of winning a fight.

The Generic Game Plan

**Imposing structure
on a fight**

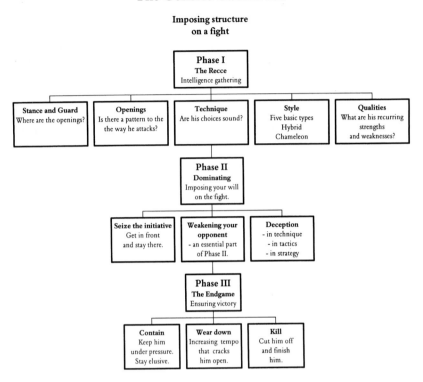

Phase I
The Recce
Intelligence gathering

Stance and Guard	Openings	Technique	Style	Qualities
Where are the openings?	Is there a pattern to the way he attacks?	Are his choices sound?	Five basic types Hybrid Chameleon	What are his recurring strengths and weaknesses?

Phase II
Dominating
Imposing your will
on the fight.

Seize the initiative	Weakening your opponent	Deception
Get in front and stay there.	- an essential part of Phase II.	- in technique - in tactics - in strategy

Phase III
The Endgame
Ensuring victory

Contain	Wear down	Kill
Keep him under pressure. Stay elusive.	Increasing tempo that cracks him open.	Cut him off and finish him.

Chart Two

Summary

In the absence of hard pre-fight information on your opponent, you must quickly gather intelligence about him. Next, you should go to work putting into effect what you have learned. Finally, you should choose the best way to end the contest – contain, wear down or kill!

The smooth blend of techniques, tactics and strategy is the hallmark of a champion. You have to know yourself and build up a picture of your opponent. You must choose the best approach to achieve dominance, and you must select the right way to bring the fight to a close.

The Specific Game Plan

Where hard information is available on your opponent – pre-fight intelligence – it is possible to create a game plan specifically geared to beating him. This pre-fight intelligence-gathering can be likened to a recce done at leisure. Without any doubt the best form of pre-fight intelligence is video footage of his previous fights.

Together with your coach, you must sit down and analyse your opponent's previous performances. You should take notes based on the generic game plan recce. Next you should draw up a list of those techniques and tactics that you perform well and that can be brought to bear against your opponent's weaknesses.

Constructing a Winning Plan

Assuming you have identified the type of fighter he is, you must construct your game plan using a three-point method: expose his weaknesses, negate his strengths, and seize and retain the initiative.

Expose his Weaknesses

Exposing his weaknesses means recognising the deficiencies in his attack and defence and bringing to bear techniques that punish these errors.

Negate his Strengths

Negating his strengths means working out precise counters to his preferred weapons and punishing him every time he tries to use them. Counter early before the technique develops its power. Counter late when he thinks he is on target. Counter his set up for the technique by blasting him with a stop-hit.

Seize and Retain the Initiative

This means beating him not only to the punch, but also to the thought. Feel him, sense what he is going to do, then jump all over his preparations. Play with your own timing and distance and strike hard. Go passive when he wants to fight and active when he wants to rest. Get ahead and stay there!

Reversing the Flow: Seizing Control of a Losing Fight

Coming from behind to win a contest is one of the hardest tasks that can confront a kick boxer. It means that you have lost your way and are getting punished for it. Sometimes this is obvious, for example, after sustaining a knock-down or after a series of rounds where you have been taken to the cleaners.

The duration of the fight and the point at which you realise that you are trailing are crucial, but one thing is certain: the amount of time left to reverse the flow will be dwindling. In these circumstances, the first question you must ask yourself is 'Why is this happening?' The second question is 'How do I reverse the flow and climb back into the driving seat?'

If you are losing a fight, somehow, someway, you are going to have to adapt. To do that you have to quickly identify those elements of your opponent's style and methods that are proving successful. On the flipside, you must also ask yourself what you are doing that is making it so easy for your opponent to win.

The big question here is 'Why is this happening?' The answer to this is not simple. That your opponent is doing his job better than you is obvious, but what he is doing is not necessarily one single identifiable thing. He may be dominating for many reasons: superior speed, power, clever timing, better distance appreciation, technique, tactical choices or a superior game plan.

Despite the pain, despite the frustration, you must now be ultra-cool and isolate the reasons why he has gained an edge over you. It cannot be emphasised enough that now is the time to listen to the cool heads in the corner – your trainer and helpers are not getting hit and therefore can offer sound, objective advice. If you don't trust your corner to give you such vital information when you need it most, then you are in the wrong camp.

Whatever the elements of your opponent's style that are proving decisive against you, you must appreciate that it is being governed by his decision-making ability. He is confident and trusts his skills to do the job. Destroying this confidence should be at the heart of your fightback plan.

If you have identified the elements that are defeating you, next set about disrupting the status quo. Let's illustrate this by looking at some effective ways of neutralising these elements or stopping them altogether.

Speed – you've read about it previously and you're about to read it again: speed has three elements.

1) Limb speed: the speed at which your arm or leg moves in attack or defence. To overcome superior limb speed either move back and keep your opponent at a distance with in-line kicks such as front and side kicks, or move in to close range, which will reduce limb-speed advantage to manageable levels.

2) Body speed: this boils down to footwork and can be defined as the ability to move in and out of range rapidly. Fight at close range to counter it. This removes his advantage, like taking a piece from his chess game.

3) Reaction speed: this is the speed at which a fighter sees an opportunity and responds correctly. The way to defeat good reaction speed is to use plenty of feints and bluffs. It makes your opponent unwilling to take a chance and his hesitation will prevent him from taking advantage of his superior reaction speed.

Clever Timing

If you are being 'out-timed' then you have to realise that your opponent is reading you very well and is concentrating on picking his shots. To disrupt this process you must inject some random elements into your footwork and attacks.

Perhaps without realising it you always attack in the same way or with the same timing and rhythm. Start to reverse the flow by using sudden arrhythmic movement – move in and out of range rapidly and randomly. This will produce hesitation on his part. Now add to his woes by concentrating on beating him to the punch. The second he moves, blast him.

Also try rushing him suddenly and roughing him up. There is nothing like a couple of good body shots to do this. Pain is a great respect-getter.

Better Distance Appreciation

Your opponent will have a preferred fighting range. If he's a kicker he will want you at long range; if he's a body puncher, he'll want you at short range.

The most obvious course is to fight at the opposite range to the one that he prefers. But you should also occasionally pick your moment to fight from his preferred range, say after having caught him with some good shots, because nothing will freak him out more than being 'served up' on what he feels is his own ground.

Technique

There are two ways of dealing with a particularly troublesome technique when you are on the receiving end. Either stop your opponent from throwing it, or turn a vice into a virtue.

If your opponent is hitting you regularly then first adjust your distance, then adjust your timing. These two in conjunction will spoil the shot, but you can add to its demise by good footwork and upper body movement. For example, if it's a roundhouse kick that is causing the problem, then circle away from its power. If it's a fast jab then use head movement to prevent the clean hit.

Turning a vice into a virtue means letting your opponent throw his favourite technique, and then countering him with a hard, punishing combination so that he loses faith in the very thing that is working for him. This calls for good perception and anticipation so that you can jump all over him the second you see the set-up.

Tactical Choice

Tactical choice is strongly related to fighting style. Your opponent will want to conduct the fight under his own terms and will select the range and pace at which he wants to fight you. Remember that opposites cancel out, thus legs are cancelled by hands, close range by distance, movement by containment, rhythm by randomness. In fighting terms this means imposing not so much your own choices, but rather the ones that make your opponent less effective.

Game Plan

Game plans are the hardest thing to disrupt. They are the product of the homework the opposition has done on you. They may have watched videos, seen you fight or received insider information on your fighting style. They have gone away and have come up with a tight plan that aims to put you on the rack and keep you there. The answer to being on the receiving end of a tight game plan is harassment.

You must jolt him from the game plan by unsettling him in as many departments as you can. Do this by attacking his balance with sweeps, pushes, and laying-on. Next, play with the timing and distance. Then use randomness to disrupt his decision-making. Rough him up, back him up and beat him up.

Keep him on the back foot mentally and physically so that he is reacting to you rather than concentrating on his mission. In short, you must become the bee in his ear, denying him the physical and mental space to work effectively.

Summary

There are many fights which I could quote as a good example of reversing the flow, but the one that sticks in my mind occurred a few years ago. It was scheduled as a seven-rounder between Chris Wotton and Bertil Queely.

The fight started quickly, and Queely put himself in the driving seat with heavy clubbing punches and strong, fast kicks. Wotton was obviously taken aback by the strength and ferocity of the assault, and by the end of round two the crowd was waiting for the knockout.

That was when Wotton turned the fight on its head. The first thing he did was use straight punches and kicks to keep Queely out of range. Then he gradually turned up the heat and rocked

Queely with some impressive-looking techniques. Finally he stopped Queely in the fourth.

It says a lot about both the character of Wotton and the savvy of his trainer Steve Kerridge that between them they turned disaster into triumph. It will not surprise you to learn that Wotton went on to win a version of the world title.

Finally a fitting quote from Mexican revolutionary Emiliano Zapata:

'Do nothing you are expected to do, do everything that nobody expects you to do, keep cover, shoot straight and never let up.'

Part Four: Deconstructing the Champion

What makes a champion? What is the difference between an experienced hard-working professional fighter who reaches the upper levels of the sport and the man that travels the extra mile? What marks out such a man? What are his qualities? What are his skills? What are his physical and mental attributes? Can you obtain the necessary qualities through sheer hard work? Does luck play a part? Or is there an X-factor – an indescribable something that cannot be quantified? Are champions born or can they be made?

The aim of this book is to guide you onto the path of a world title by teaching you the higher levels of kick boxing skill. To this end we will now attempt our hardest task yet, the deconstruction of that most fabulous of beasts, the champion, or to be more precise – the world champion. And to do that we have to look at the ultimate fighter.

One-Eyed Men

'In the Country of the blind the one-eyed man is king.'
– H. G. Wells

This quote should produce a few red faces out there, for its meaning in a kick boxing sense is quite clear: if the opposition is weak, anyone can gain a victory. Or to put it another way, owning a dog-eared, nondescript, unrecognised title by beating sub-standard opposition means nothing more than being a 'one-eyed man'.

A few flashy techniques, a strong right hand, the ability to take a punch – these are all capable of earning you a sub-standard title. God knows enough of these are won every weekend at shows around the United Kingdom, Europe and the United States.

These pseudo-champions are everywhere and come in some amazing forms – national champions who have had less than ten fights, continental champions who have never fought anybody outside their own country, and world champions who have never fought anybody outside their own continent.

My purpose though is not to attack these people for the hell of it, but merely to define the genuine article – the ultimate fighter. The ultimate fighter is a totally different character from the pseudo-champion. At the very least he is a man who has paid his dues, attained a high skill level, overcome anyone who stood in his way nationally and was prepared to journey abroad and face the toughest opposition to be found there.

There are such people in all countries, but what is it that they possess that puts them head and shoulders above the rest? Is there a checklist that you can train for and mark off as steps to greatness? Can you reach the top rung – a World Championship?

The Ultimate Fighter

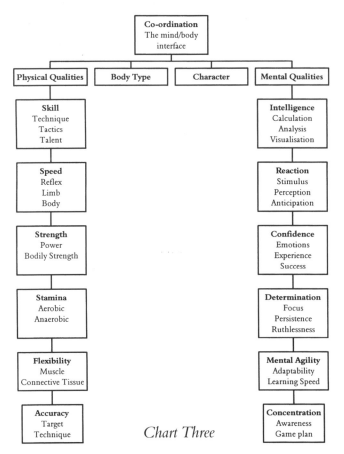

Chart Three

The Ultimate Fighter

'Lucky? Yes, I find the more I practise, the luckier I get!'
– Gary Player, South African golfer

Whether you currently hold a title or have been fighting for some time, you need to acquire a keen appetite for skill, knowledge and fitness if you are to maximise your chances of going on to a world title.

Genuine world titles are hard things to acquire and harder still to keep. There is a saying: 'A journey of a thousand miles begins with the first step.' Basically, you've got to start somewhere. We will start by deconstructing a champion.

Chart Three is a breakdown of the requirements for becoming an ultimate fighter. It's a daunting list. Though the word 'list' is, perhaps, not the best description of what is shown. 'Recipe' would be more accurate, for the various parts have to be measured, blended and then 'cooked' so that they produce the finished result.

As you read through this section and match it against the chart, you should reflect on where you are now and what qualities you need to acquire in your quest. Honesty and acute analysis are called for. Let us start by examining the physical qualities.

The Physical Qualities of a Champion

The physical qualities of a champion fall into six main categories: skill, speed, strength, stamina, flexibility and accuracy, each of which has various components.

1) Skill
Technique

All potential champions should acquire not only a good range of techniques, but also variations on the standard techniques. These variations are used whenever you can gain an advantage or need to negate your opponent's success. Never forget that fifty per cent of fighting is not getting hit. Work defensive skills until they are second nature.

To acquire technique, focus on repetition, analysis and supplementary training.

• Work the technique until it is fast, strong and accurate. Remember, 'An amateur practises until he gets it right – a professional practises until he doesn't get it wrong.'

• Analyse the technique and eliminate all unnecessary actions. Streamline for power and speed. Note your deficiencies and work on them – if you don't, your opponent will. A good coach is essential to this process. You must trust both his judgement and his character – if you have doubts about either then you are in the wrong camp. A coach cannot turn a pig's ear into a silk purse, but he should be capable of bringing out the best in you.

• Supplementary training involves work on the bag, pads, shields, weights, speed ball and jump rope, as well as shadow-boxing practice. Each area of skill needs to be examined, tested and refined. Blunt tools are dangerous.

Tactics

Tactics are how you apply your techniques, bringing your sharpest weapons against your opponent's weakest edge. For example, using speed and footwork to offset and confuse a stronger opponent; ambushing and beating up a weaker, but more skilful opponent; using superior kicking techniques to keep a puncher at long range. When skills are equal, the man who applies tactics the most effectively will win.

Talent

This is inborn skill. A natural ability to take commonplace techniques to a higher level. When pure talent is married to hard work, the result can produce the ultimate fighter. There is a saying: 'If you want an Olympic gold medal, first get the right parents.'

Body type is a serious factor here. You may want to be a heavy puncher, but if you are long and skinny, you may have to settle for snap rather than power. Equally, if you are short and inflexible you may never achieve the ability to throw knockout head kicks.

2) Speed

Reflex Speed

Quickness of the eye is of the utmost importance to a kick boxer. Seeing the threat or the opportunity faster than your opponent can give you a fight-winning edge. Remember, it takes 5,000 repetitions to turn a physical action into an instantaneous reflex.

Limb Speed

Another way of saying technique. To attain real limb speed is relatively easy – repetition, repetition, repetition! Do not underestimate the body's ability to learn. One of the chief reasons for fighters failing to achieve their maximum potential is the lack of will power to drive themselves on through the hours of endless repetition necessary to attain world champion skills.

Body speed

In a nutshell, footwork. You must close the gap quickly to attack or the opportunity will be lost. Equally, you must accelerate out of danger. Time must be given over to practising footwork. Together with your coach, devise some drills and build them into your schedule.

3) Strength

Bodily strength

Comes by way of your parents (body type) and should be routed through a good weight-training gym. Raw strength is what you are after, not looking good. Never underestimate the value of strength. When all other qualities are equal, the strongest man will win.

Power

Often confused with strength, but power is actually applied strength. Put simply, it is your ability to focus your bodily strength into your techniques. Hit hard! The big bag should be visited three times a week as a minimum. Work your kicks on shields to produce a blend of power and mobility.

4) Stamina
Aerobic Fitness
The last man standing is the winner! Aerobic fitness is vital for a kick boxer. In order to win, you must be in condition to use your fighting skills to their maximum throughout the duration of the fight.

The best way for a kick boxer to attain aerobic fitness is running. Long, slow distance will give you a base, *fartlek* will introduce speed, hill work and steps build raw leg power, and interval work will give you the icing on the cake. Research these terms and apply vigorously! (Go back and read *Kick Boxing – A Framework for Success*, Chapter 8.)

Anaerobic Fitness
Perhaps best described as local muscle endurance – the ability to continually rep with a set of weights is one example of this. If your muscles tire then your own body will fight against you. A kick boxer should use light weights and many reps to attain anaerobic fitness. Specialist routines can sometimes yield very positive results. (See *Combat Kick Boxing*, Chapter 13.)

5) Flexibility

Muscular Flexibility

The greater the range of movement in your limbs, the greater mechanical efficiency you will attain. Muscular flexibility is vital for greater extension, higher kicks, rapid spins and more mobility.

Connective Tissue

Ligaments and tendons also need to be pliable. If you train too rapidly with weights your muscles may respond, but leave your connective tissue trailing. This is the perfect recipe for injury. Train steadily and evenly and your connective tissue will keep pace.

6) Accuracy
Identify the Targets

You must accurately identify the targets within the fleeting moments that they come online. Striking out and hoping is redundant for a champion.

Accurate Delivery of Technique

The ability to deliver the technique on target is vital. In the opening rounds of a fight all fighters are accurate. The champion is able to maintain accuracy throughout the contest. Live on the focus pads and the floor-to-ceiling ball and work 'on the clock'.

The Mental Qualities of a Champion

This is the software that makes the machine work. These can and should be trained as much as the physical qualities. The higher you aim, the more you must train your mental qualities. In all areas of human activity the sharper man wins. *Homo sapiens* were more intelligent than the stronger Neanderthals and replaced them. The mental qualities of a champion fall into six main categories: intelligence, reaction, confidence, determination, mental agility and concentration.

1) Intelligence
Calculation
This means reading your opponent and adapting your techniques and tactics accordingly. Be cold, be certain and be ruthless.

Analysis
Deconstruct your performance in the gym and the ring. Progress can be measured better if you are methodical. Keep a training diary. Video both fights and training sessions and review them during rest periods – strengths and weaknesses will be revealed.

Visualisation
This means mental rehearsal. Study your opponent; see yourself making him miss, then land with a match-winning combination. Do this with all areas of concern when confronting a strong opponent. Rehearse your victory. The concept of recognition-primed decision-making is the key to visualisation. If you imagine your opponent's techniques coming towards you, you can rehearse your response and thus pounce on him when you recognise what he is about to do.

2) Reaction

Stimulus

The trigger that sparks off your reaction. Slow, switched-off fighters get ambushed. The latter stages of a fight are often the proof of the sharper man!

Perception

Intuitive recognition or mental sensitivity. It is your built-in radar. Switch it on and keep it on.

Anticipation

Priming the reaction. The reward for reading your opponent correctly, also called beating him to the punch. Reaction and visualisation are interdependent.

3) Confidence
Emotions

These are the chariot horses! Steer them, control them – they will lead you to victory or defeat. See *Ben Hur* for a fuller example!

Experience

Know yourself and you can fight a hundred battles without defeat. Quite simply, what has gone before is an indicator of where victory lies. Understand the past, rationalise it and then trust yourself. Fights – whether wins or losses – are but steps to the throne. Do not discard the lessons that have been hard-fought to learn.

Success

A winning record is the best base for confidence. Yet success doesn't just mean a winning fight: it can mean a previously successful technique or tactic. A past defeat can harbour the ingredients of future success.

4) Determination

Focus

Know what you are after. Don't waver or take your eyes off your goal. Everything is a distraction if it does not advance your cause.

Persistence

The positive view of stubbornness – sticking to the task and winning out by sheer doggedness. Think of the Greek legend of Antaeos. He was a gigantic wrestler who got up stronger every time he was thrown to the floor! This is the reasoning of winners and champions.

Ruthlessness

If you cannot summon up enough ruthlessness you have no business being in the ring.

5) Mental Agility

Adaptability

This is vital. Do not persist with ineffective tactics or techniques just because you feel comfortable with them. The man who adapts will survive. Read Darwin's *Origin of Species* for a fuller explanation.

Learning Speed

This is linked to adaptability. You must be quick in your appraisal of your opponent's abilities and techniques. The longer it takes to recognise the problems you face, the less certain victory is. Slow learners are never champions.

6) Concentration

Awareness

Remaining switched on throughout the fight is vital. Should your concentration lapse, you can be knocked out in the blink of an eye.

Game Plan

This is the ultimate aid to concentration. A sound game plan will bring you back on track when pain, fatigue and unruly emotions are taking control. It will keep you searching out your opponent's weaknesses and punishing them.

Now go back and examine Chart Three. You will see that the physical qualities parallel the mental qualities. Skill equals intelligence, speed equals reaction, strength equals confidence, stamina equals determination, flexibility equals mental agility and lastly, accuracy equals concentration.

The most obvious question thrown up by this deconstruction is 'If I acquire all these qualities, will I become a champion?' The answer, surprisingly, is no. For in order to become a champion you still need one more ingredient – the mark of greatness.

The Mark of Greatness

'Winning isn't everything – it's the only thing.'

Even if you strive to cover all the bases and become an ultimate fighter, becoming a world champion is not inevitable. Deconstructing the ultimate fighter is an exercise in logic. Champions have the ability to defy logic. They summon up victory when seemingly on the brink of disaster. They have flaws and overcome them. They suffer setbacks and rise above them. They have an outrageous belief in themselves – often a belief that onlookers don't share.

The mark of greatness is the X- factor that separates the champion from the rest. Champions need the mental and physical qualities listed in Chart Three, but they go beyond that. To become a world champion is to reach the summit. The champion fights only the top fighters, so why is it he that triumphs?

The Mark of Greatness - Analysis of a World Champion

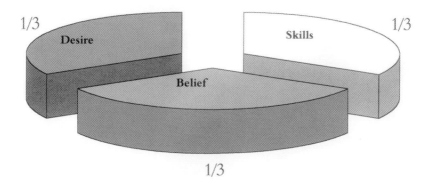

Chart Four

Look at Chart Four, 'The Mark of Greatness – Analysis of a World Champion'. Only one-third is given over to the physical and mental qualities of the ultimate fighter. To that third, two more elements must be added – belief that you can achieve, and desire that you will. To be a world champion you must transcend the ordinary, for the ordinary do not become world champions. You must rise above all others. Belief and desire are the chief indicators of the mark of greatness.

Sometimes a champion is marked out not because he has all the qualities, but because he has just one or two in abundance married to belief and desire. The great Bill Wallace was a world champion, but he was not an ultimate fighter. He did not have all the physical qualities because injury to his right leg prevented him. He did not, however, see that as a barrier to success, but a springboard!

When his injury prevented development as an ultimate fighter he simply set about working his left leg until he could throw hard, fast, deceptive kicks in combinations that simply bewildered the opposition.

We are now back to the fact that in order to become a world champion you must grow. Clearly Bill Wallace grew – nothing was going to stop him. Belief and desire made him focus on what he could do rather than what he couldn't. How many would have simply said 'My injury prevents me from becoming a champion'? Belief and desire – that's what made him a world champion and what could make *you* a champion.

Belief doesn't mean blind faith in yourself. It means trusting yourself to do the work, to make the journey despite hardship, setbacks, pain, illness and losses.

Many years ago, when I was in the Junior Leaders (a branch of the army that trained 15 to 17-year-olds to become warrant officers prior to joining the army as adults) there was a training department called the External Leadership Wing. This training involved rock climbing, pot holing, abseiling, orienteering, canoeing, trekking and mountain craft. The idea was to stretch you as an individual and find out what your true qualities were under pressure. As you walked into the training wing there was a sign. It said simply: 'The aim of this Wing is to find out how you react to fear, fatigue, hunger and cold.'

I remember only too well the sobering effect that bald statement had on me. It was in fact a challenge – a challenge that couldn't be ducked, a challenge that tested me and forced me to grow.

I don't intend to recount stories here, but take it from me, there were some severe challenges along the way and I had to dig deep to overcome them. I had to grow in the same way that you have to grow if you are to be a world champion.

Part Five deals with setting you on the right road to becoming a world champion, but now I'd like to examine someone who for me is the best example to illustrate my point.

Of all the champions that have emerged in kick boxing, one man stands out as both an ultimate fighter and a world champion. He is Benny 'The Jet' Urquidez. No one else comes near him. He simply had it all and then some. Technically he was superb, but he was also an aggressive thinker. He was a great karateka before he switched to kick boxing, so he had a solid technical base. But he realised that he would have to change his fighting style for the ring, so he set about achieving the additional skills and techniques required. He fought under any and all rules systems – fought anybody that cared to challenge him – journeyed throughout the USA, went to Europe and Asia, took on the best and won.

He was talented, technical and tough. A shining example of what can be achieved when the belief and desire meet the ultimate fighter. There are so many of his victories that I could point to that show his class and ability, yet the fight that stands out for me was his 'war' with Ian Sprung. Sprung was a big, rough, tough, never-say-die fighter who refused to be beaten and 'The Jet' had to dig deep to find the means to grind out the victory. There was nothing fancy or spectacular about this fight. It was won by Benny's belief in himself and his desire to win no matter what.

Part Five: The Structure for Success

In the concluding part of the book we will set out a structure by which you can assess where you are now, and explain how to focus your fighting career both in the gym and the ring to maximise your chances of becoming a world champion.

Many of the things that I have to say are self-explanatory whereas others are more controversial. I can only ask you to trust me and try them. My knowledge is gleaned from twenty-eight years' involvement with kick boxing as a fighter, a trainer, a judge, a referee and now as a TV commentator. In that time I have seen and analysed more champions – cabbages *and* kings – than I can honestly remember.

I believe I know what it is that makes a world champion, and I have isolated the component parts. As you read through this set of requirements, you must bring one all-important quality with you – honesty. Without it this process – this book – is without value. Remember, 'Flowers don't bloom in the dark.'

Core Skills

An analysis of the most used and most accessible kick boxing techniques will reveal that the following techniques head the list: jab, cross, left hook, rear roundhouse, lead front kick, lead leg side kick, backthrust kick, basic sweep.

These are the core skills. They comprise 90 per cent of offensive kick boxing techniques. You must master them and their variations. You must work them until they are second nature and can be produced at the moment of greatest need whilst under the greatest pressure – not in a relaxed gym environment, but at climatic moments in a meaningful must-win fight.

By all means work on your 360-degree jumping spinning backthrust, but remember that the core skills will bring you victories in more than 95 per cent of your fights. Speed, power, subtlety and accuracy are the qualities that must be continually worked.

Inventory of Personal Skills

We will begin by asking you to carry out an inventory of your present skills, knowledge and capabilities. You must be honest, because if you build on sand, your house will collapse. Use Chart Three and mark off where you believe you are currently. Circle the areas of your greatest deficiencies. Next, list the priorities and build them into your advanced fighter's training structure.

Advanced Fighter's Training Structure

You need to work on three areas: the elimination of deficiencies using a realistic schedule to improve; honing your best weapons with precision training and adding refinement; and the acquisition of additional skills and knowledge so that you grow into a champion.

Long Term: One to Three Years
- More stamina. Sustainable and measurable increase in aerobic and anaerobic fitness.
- More speed. Repetition and reaction training.
- More power. Regular and sustained periods on the big bag across the range of offensive techniques.
- Additional techniques. The acquisition of additional tools that will enhance your fighting ability.
- Tactical variety. Maturing into a sophisticated Hybrid or Chameleon.

Review after six months and then restructure and reschedule. Monitor and record all areas of training.

Middle Term: Three to Six Months
- Specific combinations. Knockouts, weakeners, economical point-scorers.
- Specialised running routines. Hill, steps and interval running.
- Specific weight training routines. Killer routine, plyometrics.
- Mobility enhancement. Greater control of movement and distance appreciation.

General honing of fighting skills and physical capabilities. Video after one, three and six months to reveal the levels of improvement.

Short Term: Six to Eight Weeks
- Creation of a specific fight game plan.
- Focus on opponent's strengths and weaknesses.
- Address perceived weaknesses and strengths in your own game.
- Rehearse specific techniques and tactics relevant to your opponent.

Schedule for a World Title

Having read all that has gone before, you now need a credible path for advancement. Just because you want a world title and feel that you are ready is insufficient. You have to convince the sanctioning bodies that you have a fair claim as a serious contender.

Depending on where you are now, you have to see regional, national and continental titles as staging posts. Not every fight can be a title fight; other people will be jostling for position as well. You may have to take non-title fights, both to keep busy and to buy credibility.

Your choice of opponent should have but two aims:
1) Improving your skills under fire.
2) Improving your ranking and status.

Improving Your Skills Under Fire

Ideally you and your coach should earmark possible opponents that you will learn from without stepping out of your class before you are ready. The gain must be balanced against the loss – too much, too soon and you could suffer a dent in your credibility. Too little, too late will be seen as next to useless – no one enjoys seeing a one-sided match. Ideally your opponents should be technically competent, but not too dangerous – and that is a hard thing to balance.

Improving Your Ranking and Status

There are opponents – maybe ex-champions or people in a similar position to yourself – who whilst not in the top flight, nevertheless have credibility. These people can advance your status in the eyes of the sanctioning body. Draw up a list of opponents and prioritise them. Next, set your sights on an intermediate title and study the holder. Go and see him fight, buy videos of his performances, make a detailed study of his strengths and weaknesses, and draw up a game plan.

Occasionally title matches fall through due to illness or injury to a challenger. The promoter will have to hunt for a substitute and may well come knocking on the door of a man not normally considered – you. The temptation to accept in these circumstances is fraught with danger – you may not get another chance if you say no, and you may get knocked out if you say yes. However, if you have this champion on your hit list and have an embryonic game plan you could just pull off an upset. You need to examine your track record and ranking. Plan a schedule of preferred fights. Target particular fighters and aim for intermediate titles. Next, broaden your knowledge and skill base by reading books and magazine articles on kick boxing and boxing, fitness and sports performance, and strategy and tactics. Two classic books are *Go Rin No Sho* – the *Book of Five Rings* by Miyamoto Musashi and *Ping Fa* – *The Art of War* by Sun Tzu. Translations of each are available from any bookshop.

The last two suggestions may seem a little off the wall, but believe me, there is serious value in them. You have to develop a hunger for knowledge about kick boxing and any sports-based skills that might assist your title challenge. If you want to break away from the crowd then you have to think laterally. Remember: 'If you always do what you always did, then you will always get what you always got!'

There is a powerful method of thinking laterally, a way of changing what you do. It's called visualisation and it is a tool used by top athletes the world over.

Visualisation: The Winning Mind

Visualisation is the mental focus that yields the best in you. It is a mental rehearsal of the skills and plans that an athlete uses in their particular field – in your case kick boxing. It allows you to develop fast reactions and the correct responses under pressure.

The application of skills, especially new skills, is frequently hindered by thinking time. If an opportunity arises to use a particular skill, your response time may see the window of opportunity close.

What mental rehearsal allows you to do is switch on your recognition-primed decision-making and beat him to the punch. You see what you have mentally rehearsed – your opponent's technique coming at you – and you see yourself evading, blocking or parrying the attack and delivering an effective response.

Similarly, when your opponent disturbs his guard and an opportunity to attack opens up, you throw the mentally rehearsed perfect attack; for example, when he allows his guarding rear hand to fall, you launch a stunning left hook to the jaw.

Each and every counter can be mentally rehearsed so that you develop lightning-fast responses to openings in his defences. The split-second chain of events unleashed by mental rehearsal is: recognition-primed decision + awareness + reaction = the perfect response.

The same process can be used to develop techniques in all aspects of training, from visualising control of fights right through to rehearsing an entire game plan for a specific fight. Post-training and pre-fight are the times to switch on the winning mind.

Method of Practice

1) Sit in a relaxed position and steady your breathing by taking slow and regular breaths.

2) Choose a particular aspect of fighting that you wish to rehearse.

3) Picture the whole exchange between you and your opponent. You should see your attack or counter smash home to the point of seeing your opponent fall.

4) All this should happen slowly. Concentrate as you would when learning a new skill and emphasise each piece of the action – footwork – release of the technique – body curve – striking the target.

5) Do this ten times.

Make visualisation a regular part of your post-training recovery. This type of mental training yields big results if you are having a particular problem with a sparring partner's attacks in the gym. It will enable you to respond effectively.

The big pay-off is that with practice you can switch on visualisation in between rounds whilst you are sitting on your stool. The next round will surprise the hell out of an opponent who up until that point has climbed all over you with a particular technique or combination.

Make visualisation part of your life and it can yield major results – and not just in the kick boxing ring. It is not daydreaming, it is not fantasy, it is a rehearsal for success.

The Process of Transformation

Throughout this book you have been asked to transform the way you see yourself, the way you train and the way you fight – all for the purpose of becoming a world champion. The process of transformation must have a beginning, therefore we have reached decision time and there remains just one last question to ask: have you got it in you to become a world champion?

If the answer is yes, then I say good hunting, and may your efforts meet an equal reward.

Pat O'Keeffe

By the same author:

Kick Boxing

Combat Kick Boxing

www.summersdale.com